Teaching the

MIDDLE AGES

With Magnificent Art Masterpieces

By Bobbi Chertok,
Goody Hirshfeld, and
Marilyn Rosh

S C H O L A S T I C
PROFESSIONAL BOOKS

New York • Toronto • London • Auckland • Sydney
Mexico City • New Delhi • Hong Kong

DEDICATED TO OUR CHILDREN
- *who helped test our art programs,*
- *who inspired us, and*
- *who continue to do so.*

ACKNOWLEDGMENTS
to the libraries of Pearl River, Nanuet, and New City,
New York for their invaluable assistance

Cover design by Norma Ortiz
Cover and Poster art: Très Riches Heures, October © Giraudon/Art Resource;
The Bayeux Tapestry © Erich Lessing/Art Resource;
Stained Glass Windows © Sonia Halliday and Laura Lushington;
The Tournament © Cliché Bibliothèque nationale de France, Paris
Interior illustration by Mona Mark
Interior design by Sydney Wright
ISBN: 0-590-64435-1

Table of Contents

About Living Art Seminars

In 1973 Bobbi Chertok, Goody Hirshfeld, and Marilyn Rosh created Living Art Seminars, a nonprofit organization designed to bring fine art into the classroom through a variety of programs. Its goal is to make art fresh, fun, and relevant to each and every child. Thousands of elementary school children and their teachers have awakened to a new appreciation of art through Living Art Seminars.

As part of the Living Arts Seminars, students and teachers visit the Metropolitan Museum of Art, where they discover the excitement and beauty of art. The seminars are also designed to help students develop respect for and understanding of different cultures, as well as stimulate students' critical-thinking skills with emphasis on observing, sequencing, listening, and reasoning. As a writer for *The New York Times* observed, "With the help of Living Art Seminars, students are discovering that art is a lot closer and more fun than they had ever imagined." Over the years Living Art Seminars has received numerous state and local grants.

In 1992 the founders of Living Art Seminars captured some of their time-tested techniques in the book *Meet the Masterpieces: Strategies, Activities, and Posters to Explore Great Works of Art*. Published the following year, *Meet the Masterpieces: Learning About Ancient Civilizations Through Art* focuses on eight ancient cultures. *Month-by-Month Masterpieces*, published in 1996, highlights ten significant artists and works of art, one for each month of the school year. *Teaching American History With Art Masterpieces* was published in 1998. It features posters, reproducible newspapers, and innovative activities to explore eight key events in American history. All are published by Scholastic Professional Books.

Introduction

*T*his book is designed to bring your students back in time 1,000 years to make the people and events of the period between 1060 to 1460 come alive. Using four magnificent works of art from the Middle Ages, the book highlights a time of castles and cathedrals by introducing students to the everyday lives of some medieval people. Your class will meet a Saxon knight who fought in the Battle of Hastings, a carpenter who helped build Chartres Cathedral, a scribe who wrote illuminated manuscripts, and a duchess who is hosting a tournament. As they become personally involved with the characters they meet, your students will be experiencing history from a new perspective. It is our hope that as they learn about government, trade, religion, art, science, and everyday life in Europe at the beginning of the first millennium, students will make comparisons with today's world as we embark on the second millennium.

Teaching the Middle Ages With Magnificent Art Masterpieces is divided into four sections. The featured works of art are:

❧ **The Bayeux Tapestry**   This embroidery was stitched by women shortly after October 14, 1066, the recorded date of the Battle of Hastings. This might be the first sequential, visual representation of an historic event. The section of the 230-foot-long masterpiece portrayed in this book features the Norman army advancing on horseback hurling lances against the Saxon foot soldiers who retaliate with flying axes.

❧ **The Donor Windows From Chartres Cathedral** (approximately 1210). Magnificent stained-glass windows were a medieval contribution to Gothic churches. Many windows at Chartres Cathedral were financed or donated by the local guilds or craftsmen's clubs. To honor these guilds, the lower portions of the stained-glass windows often portrayed the artisans at work. This book includes a section of a large window of blacksmiths shoeing a horse, surrounded by smaller windows depicting the trades of the shoemaker, butcher, fishmonger, carpenter, wheelwright, and apothecary.

❧ **Très Riches Heures, October** (approximately 1416). This is one page of an illuminated manuscript, a hand-painted work of art which was part of a prayer book. In the Middle Ages, the most popular books, in fact, the "best-sellers," were handmade prayer books called Book of Hours. The first part of these prayer books often included a calendar. On each page there was a painting illustrating an event appropriate to a month of the year. *Très Riches Heures* was a Book of Hours commissioned by a patron of the arts, the Duke de Berry. The month of October shows peasants sowing fall seeds. In the background is the Louvre, then the palace of King Charles V of France, and now a great museum of art.

❧ **The Tournament** (approximately 1455–60) from Duke Rene of Anjou's book *Treatise on the Form and Devising of a Tournament.* Handwritten and illustrated books in the Middle Ages were often instructional "how-to" manuscripts. There were treatises on how to follow the rules of chivalry and how to raise proper young ladies, as well as this one on how to hold and participate in a tournament, a major form of entertainment among nobility in the late Middle Ages. The illustration included portrays the exciting action of a tournament. Knights are engaged in a mock battle with blunt swords, as the tournament judges and spectators watch from above.

Each section in the book has five parts:

1. The Life and Times of . . . introduces a person from the work of art who steps out of the embroidery, stained glass, or illustrated manuscript to tell his or her story. From the Bayeux Tapestry we meet a Saxon housecarl, **Baldric** the Bold. The Stained-Glass Windows present **Modeste Ebeniste**, a carpenter. The *Très Riches Heures* is handwritten by a scribe, **Olivier Malet**. From the Tournament illustration is a duchess, **Germaine de Valery**. Each reproducible story is followed by a discussion question designed to help students compare and make connections between life in the Middle Ages and life today.

2. The Writings of . . . presents reproducible pages of personal events and historic news that take place during the lifetime of one of the medieval characters. The writings, which can be read aloud by the teacher or independently by students, also give insights into food and fashion, famous people, beliefs and superstitions, as well as facts about science and inventions during the Middle Ages. After reading this section, students may wish to write diaries or chronicles about other characters in the works of art. The four sections are the Chronicles of **Baldric**, the Manuscripts of **Modeste Ebeniste**, the Diaries of **Olivier Malet**, and the Memoirs of **Germaine de Valery**.

3. The Picture Tells a Story sections are teaching guides that feature background information about the history, style, and key elements of each work of art presented in a question-and-answer format. The questions are designed to encourage students to observe, imagine, articulate ideas, express feelings, and use critical-thinking skills. The questions also provide a great deal of information about medieval times, art and architecture, dress, social mores, occupations, trade, government, and history. Many questions are open-ended and may lead to surprising detours as students share their own interpretations of the artists' work. Students can find the answers to some of the questions in *The Writings Of . . .* section. For interested students, the questions might serve as springboards for further investigation and research.

4. Reproducible Activity Pages feature activities that encourage students to connect the ideas in the artwork to their world either in writing or through art of their own. When you distribute an activity page, review the directions with the class and encourage students to respond creatively. Each section has two reproducible activity pages.

5. Extension Activities include a variety of additional activities for you to select from to build students' critical-thinking skills and to extend the learning experience across the curriculum. Many of the activities require student research. A number of the activities can be expanded into culminating events such as a Medieval Day, a Medieval Fair, or a tournament at school.

The book has an additional bonus—a game called Richard: Yea or Nay. The game presents the life of one of the most romantic and colorful medieval kings, Richard the Lionhearted. The game board itself is a map showing the medieval world and specifically the route of the Third Crusade. The game board may be reproduced and attached to cardboard, and laminated. Since board games such as chess were a popular form of entertainment during the Middle Ages, your students may wish to create their own medieval board games about the life of a person, a battle, the siege of a castle, or other historic events.

The Life and Times
of a Saxon Housecarl, Baldric the Bold

I am a loyal member of the King's bodyguards, a professional soldier, and a defender of my country, England. To my good fortune, I am blessed with a strong body and an unbeatable spirit. When other men are filled with fear, I rush forward. I am a *housecarl*, a Scandinavian word that means "houseboy." We are called that because many of us live in the royal household during times of emergency.

Yesterday King Harold called us to duty. I have been awaiting his summons, for I am aware of the danger facing England. Duke William, the Norman, threatens us and is determined to overthrow my lord Harold. Since a housecarl must always be available for immediate service in time of war, I called my good wife, Ostritha, to me and instructed her as best I could on the duties and responsibilities of managing my small estate. Since I am often away from home, she is quite good at keeping our tenant farmers content and seeing that our fields are plowed and our livestock fed. I pray that she and our seven small children will fare well if I fall in battle.

I have laid out my armor, shield, and ax and inspected them for flaws. I have also readied my padded undergarments, which will protect against the rough chain mail I wear in battle.

I have harnessed my horse for the journey to King Harold's camp, but my horse will not be used for fighting. We English fight on foot as is proper for a well-trained army.

For those who are interested, I have kept a chronicle of the events that have led up to this day. I pray I may survive the upcoming battle and continue to write down my thoughts so my children can understand a little about life in these most unsettling times.

◆ ◆ ◆ ◆ ◆ ◆ ◆ ◆ ◆ ◆ ◆ ◆ ◆ ◆ ◆ ◆

DISCUSSION QUESTION: Baldric was steadfast in his loyalty to King Harold. To whom or to what ideas should a person give allegiance or loyalty? How might you demonstrate loyalty to your parents, to a friend, or to your country?

The Chronicles of Baldric

◆ A Time of Unrest ◆

London, England
18 November 1065

Whispers are heard up and down these Isles that King Edward the Confessor, that good and saintly man, is gravely ill. He has sat on the throne of England for 23 years, during which time he has kept our country peaceful. For the last five years I have served as housecarl to Edward. He sees that my family and I are well provided for.

I have often been in King Edward's presence. He appears a tall person with a white beard and a serious countenance.

Since the King will die, who will take his place?

◆ Our King Is Dead ◆

London, England
5 January 1066

Queen Edith, wife of Edward, has just announced the death of her husband. I, along with other loyal subjects, mourn his passing. Edith's brother, Harold Godwinson, a powerful, wealthy, and ambitious noble-man, has his eye on the throne. Harold claims that Edward, while on his deathbed, selected him as heir. With Edward dead, I offer my services to Harold.

◆ Conflict ◆

London, England
21 January 1066

News from across the Channel has reached the ears of peasant and lord alike. William, Duke of Normandy, a cousin of Edward, also lays claim to the English throne. The hot-tempered William is furious at Harold's actions since he has always con-sidered himself the next in line to rule over this great island nation. There is no way that Harold and William can resolve this matter peacefully.

Rumor has it that William is preparing to invade England. Spies confirm that he is busy directing his Norman workers to build a fleet of ships to carry knights, horses, weapons, and barrels of wine to last through the siege.

I have no doubt that I will soon be in battle.

◆ A New Star Lights the Sky ◆

London, England
30 April 1066

I cannot stop gazing up into the night sky, astonished by a mighty light with a long tail. It looks to me like a star with hair.

When first observed, many people (not I, of course) screamed with fear at the unusual sight. Some thought the end of the world was near; others thought a great dis-aster was to come. They may be right! Old men murmured that it was an omen that promised great changes in the kingdom.

10

As the days passed, we began to get used to its strange presence. Now it has gone back into the heavens from whence it came. I think it is an astronomical event of great importance. The monks who know about such things say it is called a "comet."*

* Halley's comet

◆ Normans Invade England ◆

London, England
28 September 1066

The Norman fleet has crossed the English Channel and has disembarked on the beach at Pevensey. Great fear is spreading through all of England. Normans are looting and burning Anglo-Saxon homes as they make their way to Hastings. Will my beloved England ever be the same again?

◆ Motte and Bailey Castle ◆

Hastings, England
10 October 1066

Our Saxon spies have returned to camp with news that the Norman army, which has been on English soil for only two weeks, has constructed a castle. The Normans have directed their servants to heap up mounds of earth, which they call the *motte,* and build a wooden tower on top. Next, they dug a ditch or moat around it and filled it with water. They work with great speed.

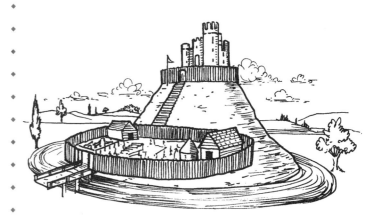

Alongside the moat they have erected a courtyard called the *bailey* where their men and horses are barricaded. Duke William has set up his household in the tower where he is planning his battle strategy. Sadly, our spies cannot penetrate their guarded moat.

◆ Saxons Defend Homeland ◆

Hastings, England
13 October 1066

It is the eve of battle. Tomorrow Duke William's Normans will confront King Harold and his Saxon army in battle. I hear that we are evenly matched for numbers of men, but the Norman soldier has the better fighting equipment. What nonsense! There is no better warrior than a heavily armed English housecarl.

The Chronicles of Baldric

⬥ The Battle of Hastings ⬥

Hastings, England
14 October 1066

Today is a brilliant autumn day. I am surrounded by trees of gold, orange, and red on Senlac Hill. What better place to defend my King and country! King Harold has positioned his housecarls in the front line of battle. I hold my shield on my left arm and together with my brave fighting companions we form a solid "shield wall."

I use my right arm to hurl my battle ax against the oncoming Normans on horseback. Our heavily armed men push them back time after time. If a housecarl falls, another quickly comes forward to fill in the gap. But we are getting tired. The force of the Norman attack seems to grow each time they charge.

Suddenly, I realize that our unbroken formation no longer exists. There is confusion. Never before had we fought against horsemen in battle. I am surrounded by Normans and return blow after blow.

I look for my King, only to learn that he has been killed. I have no time to mourn him. I join other housecarls who fight on around his body. It is with pride that I tell you that not one of Harold's personal bodyguards was taken prisoner. As dark begins to fall, I slip away into the forest. I am bloody and exhausted.

This is a sad day for us. We have lost the war. The Normans have conquered England.

⬥ William, the Conqueror, Is King

London, England
25 December 1066

Today I joined crowds of curious and worried people to see Duke William crowned King of England. French has become the language of the nobility, but the ordinary people are keeping English alive by speaking it in their homes. Life is no longer as it was.

* * * * * * * * * * *

⬥ Taillefer ⬥

London, England
12 February 1067

I have recurring dreams about the Norman minstrel, Taillefer, who acted so bravely at the Battle of Hastings.

I often think of how Taillefer pushed himself to the front of the Norman army. He was shouting tales of heroism and tossing his sword up in the air as he marched. His tricks and loud voice confused us greatly. Bravely, Taillefer rushed alone into the center of our Saxon forces. We stopped his advance with a hail of spears that killed him instantly.

I will always remember his courageous spirit.

* * * * * * * * * * *

⬥ Curfew ⬥

London, England
18 March 1068

I am much angered by the curfew which we must obey since the Normans have come to power. At sunset the curfew bell begins tolling and everyone hastens to be home by dark. The gates are drawn shut to keep out unwelcome strangers and prowling wolves.

The Chronicles of Baldric

Regardless of the cold, no fires are allowed to burn at night in any home. We are told this will prevent sparks from setting the wooden houses on fire while the occupants sleep.

Being forced to stay indoors is very hard for a warrior!

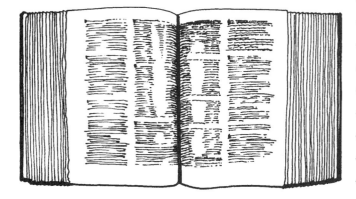

The Domesday Book

London, England
25 December 1086

I am much annoyed with King William, who is taxing me and the other landholders beyond any reasonable measure. William has sent teams of men to every part of his kingdom to write down who owns land and how much it is worth. All this information is now collected in a book called the Domesday Book. *Domesday* means "judgment." I questioned the amount I was to pay and was turned away without a hearing. This book is very unpopular and has led to outbreaks of violence throughout the land.

NEWS FROM ABROAD
The First Crusade

Clermont, France
1095

Pope Urban II traveled to Clermont from Rome to hold a conference. There, he appealed to Christian believers to rescue the holy city of Jerusalem from the hands of the Turks. They call this great journey across the world to Jerusalem a Crusade. It is considered a "holy war." Crusaders are told that if they die in their struggle to convert those who are not Christian, sins will be forgiven. The Crusade is resulting in much violence as thousands of nonbelievers are being killed.

Skiing on a Shinbone

Salisbury, England
10 January 1096

When the snow falls on the fields of my estate in winter, I have watched young men do a curious thing. They tie the shinbones of animals to their feet and use iron poles to push themselves along. I think I will try it sometime. It looks like fun.

❧ The Chronicles of Baldric ❧

✦ Sick ✦

Salisbury, England
18 February 1096

Today I awakened with a bout of chills. My head was burning with a fever and my body would not still—it shook and shook. My wife, Ostritha, did catch a frog to hang about my neck, but to no avail. Then she treated me with a broth of marigold leaves, which reduced my fever. Next, she placed a spider in a raisin which I swallowed and henceforth had a speedy recovery.

* * *

✦ Helpful Hints for a ✦ Prettier You

London, England
21 March 1097

Have you heard of Dame Trot, the woman doctor who is famous as a beauty consultant? Ostritha eagerly follows her advice. I pass on to you some of the Dame's best-known recipes.

To lose weight: Instruct your servants to bury you in the sand at the seashore.

To increase your attractiveness: Behead a lizard, boil it in oil, and rub it into a dry scalp.

For general cleanliness: Wear a fur belt when staying indoors. All the fleas and insects that live in your house will gather there. Every so often, take the belt outside and shake it with great energy, thus ridding you and your home of these annoying pests.

✦ Dining Out ✦

London, England
28 July 1097

Two fortnights ago, my friend Lord Alfric invited Ostritha and me to dinner at his castle. Naturally, I had our squire and servant Olf prepare our horses and accompany us.

Alfric and his family sat upon finely carved chairs on a raised platform in the great hall. Ostritha and I were greatly honored to be seated next to them. Before dining, we washed our hands with water poured from a beautifully decorated aquanmanile*.

Olf, who sat on a long bench at the lower table, washed his hands in a large tub and dried them on a long towel. Of course, fingers must be clean since they are used for eating.

The meat pies and leg of venison were good and we did eat much off large *trenchers*, pieces of stale bread upon which our food was placed. All the guests, including Ostritha and me, brought our own knives to cut the meat from the bone. Happily, Lord Alfric provided us with cups which his servants kept filled with cider and wine. As honored guests, Ostritha and I sat above the salt cellar that marked the division between the nobility and the common people.

* a large bowl used for washing hands

Teaching the Middle Ages With Magnificent Art Masterpieces
Scholastic Professional Books

The Bayeux Tapestry

Dimensions: 231 feet long and 20 inches high

Medium: Embroidery on linen   **Date:** Approximately 1067

◆ ◆ ◆ ◆ ◆ ◆ ◆ ◆ ◆ ◆ ◆ ◆ ◆ ◆ ◆ ◆

What is the Bayeux Tapestry? ❧

Although it is always referred to as a tapestry, it is incorrectly named. A tapestry is a picture that is woven on a loom. The Bayeux Tapestry is an embroidery which was hand-sewn on linen fabric with needle and colored woolen thread. This tapestry might be called the world's oldest comic strip since the story is told in a series of 74 continuous scenes. The fighting scene depicted above in two sections is only a small part of the whole. To impart some sense of the scale of this remarkable work, "there are 626 human figures, 190 horses, 35 dogs, 506 various other animals, 37 ships, 33 buildings and 37 groups of trees." (From *The Bayeux Tapestry* by Charles H. Gibbs-Smith. Phaidon Publishers, Inc. New York, 1973, p.6)

Who made the tapestry? ❧

The talented needle women who stitched it were almost certainly English. They completed the tapestry shortly after the Battle of Hastings, which took place in 1066. However, there are two major theories about the people who designed and commissioned the work.

⚜ A popular theory is that Duke William of Normandy's half brother commissioned an artist to design the work and arranged to have it embroidered.

⚜ Others attribute the tapestry to Matilda, the wife of King William. Legend says that although Matilda could not go into battle at her husband's side, she could gather her ladies, and together they used their many-colored threads to tell the story of William and the Norman Conquest.

Which two armies were involved in this battle?

The Anglo-Saxons and Normans confronted one another at Hastings. The Anglos and Saxons were both tribes that originally came from the north of Europe and invaded the English isles. The word *Saxon* comes from *seax*, the short sword they carried.

The Normans came from Normandy, which lies across the English Channel in France. *Norman* means "norseman," a medieval word for Viking.

How did the two armies differ?

The Saxon soldiers were on foot. These men were the housecarls, highly trained warriors who were part of the king's bodyguard. They were accompanied by the *fierds*, peasants who were required by their lords to join the army for two months a year. At the end of that time they could go back to their farms. They did not have armor. Locate the fierd in the tapestry.

Racing toward them from the left are the Normans on horseback. Most of the Norman soldiers were armed adventurers who were willing to risk their lives for good pay and the possibility of receiving large awards of money or land if they defeated the Saxons on English soil.

Where was the battle taking place?

The battle actually occurred on Senlac Hill, about six miles northwest of the town of Hastings, in England. Today the village where the Normans and Saxons fought is simply called Battle.

How were the fighting men dressed?

Saxons and Normans wore similar armor that was very uncomfortable. The *Hauberk* (hoe-birk) was a heavy shirt of chain-mail made by stitching wire rings together. It could weigh as much as 30 pounds. The chain mail leggings, which went down to the knees, probably had slits in the front and back to allow a knight to sit on a horse. Woolen stockings or leg bandages covered the lower portion of the leg. Each warrior carried a kite-shaped shield made of wood and leather that could protect a good portion of his body.

How were the soldier's faces protected?

A separate piece of mail called a *coif* was designed to cover the neck and head and provided an opening for the face. Atop this was placed a cone-shaped iron helmet with *nasals*—pieces of metal to protect the nose.

How did the Saxon and Norman hairstyles differ?

Although Saxon and Norman armor was similar, hairstyles were not. Normans wore their hair short and shaved the back of their heads. Their faces were clean-shaven.

Teaching the Middle Ages With Magnificent Art Masterpieces
Scholastic Professional Books

Saxons wore longer hair and beards. Locate the Saxon soldier at the front of the shield-wall with a beard poking out above his coif.

How many different weapons can you identify in this section of the tapestry? ✍

A mace flies through the air. Lances are thrown by both sides, and the small lone Saxon archer lets loose an arrow. An ax is carried by one of the soldiers in the shield-wall.

What is pictured in the lower border?
What is pictured in the upper border? ✍

The dead and dying of both sides have fallen down into the lower border of the tapestry, and therefore the border becomes an integral part of action depicted in this section.

The upper border is always more decorative and usually includes beasts both real and imaginary.

Why do you suppose there is writing on the tapestry?
Why is it in Latin? ✍

Throughout the tapestry Latin inscriptions are used as captions to clarify the events. Latin was the written and spoken language of the church at that time. CONTRA ANGLORUM EXERCITU can be translated as AGAINST THE ENGLISH ARMY.

How do you think the Norman Conquest changed England? ✍

William had promised his knights handsome rewards for fighting at the Battle of Hastings. He took away land formerly owned by Englishmen who had fought against him at Hastings and divided it among his own Norman followers. Many Normans sent home for their wives and families, and before long, French-speaking Normans were everywhere. William's wife, Matilda, was crowned queen, and in less than a year she gave birth to a son born on English soil. His name was Henry, and he would someday be the King of England. Although William came to England as a conqueror, in reality he succeeded in uniting Normans and Saxons.

Where is the tapestry today? ✍

It is now back in Bayeux Cathedral in northwestern France, but throughout its 900-year history, it has had many adventures. During the French Revolution there were stories that the tapestry was taken to be used as a wagon cover, but was miraculously saved. Later it was almost cut up to make a float for a carnival. It was in great danger during World War II when the Germans tried to remove it from France, but the tapestry always survived and remains today one of the world's most fascinating and artistic historic treasures.

The Bayeux Tapestry

· · · · · · · · · · · · · · · · · ·

1 **A Castle to Keep** In the Middle Ages, castles were built to protect a lord and his family. An entire community lived inside the castle walls. Castles included:

❧ a tower, or "keep," where the lord lived.

❧ a separate cookhouse where food was prepared.

❧ craft shops where craftsmen made necessary items such as tools and furniture.

❧ a church where the family worshipped.

❧ a bailey—the courtyard where animals were penned.

Divide the class into groups. Have each group use reference books and/or the Internet to research the structures within castle walls. Each group should design and build a castle using oatmeal boxes and other small boxes, wood, aluminum foil, paper, and pasta shapes. Castles may include towers, baileys, moats, drawbridges, and even dungeons. David MacAulay's *Castle* (Houghton Mifflin, 1982) is a wonderful resource for this project

2 **A Matter of Maps** Direct your students to use atlases to find maps that show Europe in the year 1000 A.D. Have them trace the maps, showing the towns and boundaries that existed at the time. Also tell students to indicate rivers, seas, and mountains. Then encourage students to compare their maps to maps of Europe today.

3 **Situations Wanted** The lord of a manor had many different servants with duties that were unique to the Middle Ages. Some are listed below:

Chandler: one who crafted candles

Cupbearer: a young man willing to taste all drinks to check for impurities and

18

poisons before they were offered to the lord

Laverer: a man of gentle demeanor who washed the hands of all diners before they ate

Henchman: a man willing to perform all errands and tasks desired by the lord

Almoner: a man of compassionate nature who distributed money or food to the poor on behalf of the lord

Ask students to research other jobs that laborers held in the early Middle Ages. Then have them write help-wanted ads listing the qualifications for each job.

4 **Step Out of the Tapestry** The cast of characters in the Bayeux Tapestry were real people. Have your class research Edward the Confessor, King Harold, Duke William, Bishop Odo, and Queen Matilda. Then ask them to write biographical sketches of these famous figures who influenced England in the 11th century.

5 **Mind Your Manners** The Norman and Saxon lords hosted banquets in the great halls of their castles. Proper table manners indicated that you were true nobility. Here are some medieval rules of etiquette:

⚜ Don't stick your fingers in your ears.

⚜ Don't scratch your head at the table.

⚜ Don't put bones back on your dish. Instead drop them on the floor.

⚜ Avoid spitting and belching.

⚜ Don't put your fingers in the food at the same time as your neighbor does.

Suggest that your students plan a medieval banquet. Stale bread can be used as plates (trenchers), and the only utensil that can used is a spoon. Tell students to research possible menus and to draw up a set of acceptable table manners. Form committees and charge them with planning entertainment and setting up the banquet. Entertainment might include jugglers, musicians, acrobats, minstrels, and poets. For more information about medieval food, look for Boke of Gode Cookery a Web site (www.labs.net/dmccormick/hven.htm), which is filled with fascinating facts and recipes.

◆ ◆ ◆ ◆ ◆ ◆ ◆ ◆ ◆ ◆ ◆ ◆ ◆ ◆ ◆ ◆ ◆ ◆ ◆ ◆

Answers to *The Battle That Changed England* (page 21)

1. This distance across the English Channel at St. Valery is shorter than at Bayeux.

2. Supplies could be shipped on the Sommes River and taken to the English Channel for transport to England.

3. A motte is a mound of earth on which a wooden tower is built. A moat is built around it and filled with water. Soldiers and horses live in the barricaded courtyard called a bailey. A motte and bailey castle offers good defensive protection.

History on the Move

On the Bayeux Tapestry the story of the Battle of Hastings is told in sequential order, much like a comic strip.

Recall an historical event, and illustrate it in the central panel. In the left-hand panel, draw the situation that caused the event; in the right-hand panel, draw the effect. Enhance your illustrated story by drawing the appropriate symbols in the borders above and below. Color your drawing.

Teaching the Middle Ages With Magnificent Art Masterpieces
Scholastic Professional Books

The Battle That Changed England

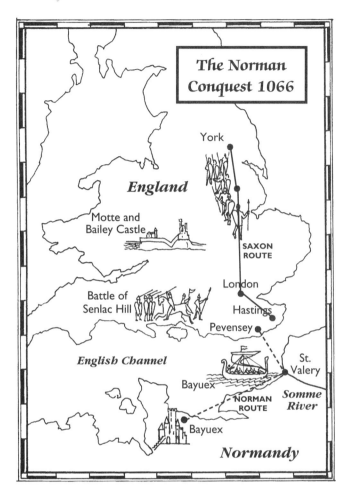

The Norman
Conquest 1066

York

England

Motte and
Bailey Castle

SAXON
ROUTE

London

Battle of
Senlac Hill

Hastings

Pevensey

English Channel

St.
Valery

Bayuex

Somme
River

NORMAN
ROUTE

Bayuex

Normandy

In the chart below, compare the routes of the Normans and the Saxons. Write your answers in the appropriate boxes.

	Normans	Saxons
Points of departure		
Transportation		
Direction in which they traveled		

Legend

Saxon Route ————

Norman Route ------

What Do You Think?

1. Crossing the English Channel is often dangerous. Why did the Normans travel to St. Valery and use this place as a point of departure? _____

_____

2. Locate the Somme River. How did this river aid the Normans in getting their supplies from the mainland? _____

_____

3. What is a motte and bailey castle? Why did the Normans build one when they arrived on English soil? _____

_____

The Life and Times
of a Carpenter, Modeste Ebeniste

*T*he monks often tell the story of how I came to live with them. Brother Gaston was working in the herb garden of the monastery when he heard a strange cry. Fearing a wild beast had climbed over the walls, he grabbed his wooden rake for protection and cautiously went to investigate. To his surprise he found a basket containing a screaming infant boy—me! The monks named me Modeste and from that day on the monastery became my home.

I tried hard to please the monks, but to tell the truth, I was always getting in trouble. I was not the only child in the monastery. Many rich families sent their sons there to get an education, and these boys never seemed to have any difficulty following the rules and regulations.

At mealtimes in the dining room we all had to eat in silence while we listened to a reading from the Bible. As soon as the reader began, I would get this terrible urge to scratch my back or wiggle my nose. But the most difficult thing for me was to keep my mouth shut. I can't tell you how many times I broke the silence with a giggle or a yawn. Then I would be dragged out of the refectory in disgrace and punished for my behavior. It soon became clear that I was not suited to the monastic life.

However, I did have a talent that the monks recognized and encouraged. I took great delight in carving objects out of wood. When one of the monks' bedpost broke, I found the right piece of wood and mended it. I also carved a crude but recognizable image of Brother Gaston's patron saint.

For such efforts the monks allowed me to stay on until my 12th birthday, when I was apprenticed to a master of the carpenters' guild in the city of Chartres. He taught me the craft to which I have devoted my life.

◆ ◆ ◆ ◆ ◆ ◆ ◆ ◆ ◆ ◆ ◆ ◆ ◆ ◆ ◆ ◆ ◆

DISCUSSION QUESTION: During the Middle Ages there were a limited number of jobs. Usually a boy was trained to do what his father had done before him. Craftsmen's work was strictly regulated by guilds. Very few jobs were open to women. How has this changed today? What are some of the ways in which people prepare for careers today?

Teaching the Middle Ages With Magnificent Art Masterpieces
Scholastic Professional Books

The Manuscripts of Modeste Ebeniste

NEWS FROM ABROAD
✦ Jerusalem Captured ✦

Jerusalem
10 April 1187

News has just come from the East that Jerusalem has been overwhelmed by a Moslem army led by the famed warrior, Saladin, sultan of Egypt and Syria. After 88 years of mostly Christian rule the holy city is once again in Arab hands. So be it! I, for one, would rather stay at home where I belong.

NEWS FROM ENGLAND
✦ King Richard Leads ✦ Crusade

London, England
3 September 1189

Word has reached France that on this day Richard I, whom they call the Lionhearted, was crowned the King of England. He is beginning to raise an army to march to the Holy Land and rescue Jerusalem. Another Crusade has begun!

Most of the great lords of Europe are also ready to risk everything in the East. But it is men like me who are being taxed to pay for this venture.

✦ Minstrel's Melody ✦ Rescues King Richard

Durrenstein Castle, Austria
11 July 1193

We Frenchmen are always curious about the events that take place in England—land of our long-time enemies. Travelers to England are returning with strange stories of betrayal and disloyalty. While Richard was busy organizing the Crusade, his brother John began plotting to name himself King.

Learning that his life was in danger, Richard disguised himself as a pilgrim. As he traveled through Austria, his true identity was discovered when an alert guard spotted the royal ring on his finger.

Richard was seized by the Austrian Duke Leopold and thrown into a dungeon in Durrenstein Castle.

For more than a year the King's English countrymen had no idea where he was. According to a story I recently heard, it was Richard's companion, the minstrel Blondel, who found him.

Blondel had traveled all over Europe singing a song that he and Richard had written as youths. He hoped that Richard would recognize the song and respond. That is exactly what happened! When Blondel reached Durrenstein Castle, Richard, still imprisoned within its walls, heard the song from his childhood and happily joined in. After claiming a huge ransom worth 35 tons of silver, Duke Leopold allowed Richard to return to England.

◆ Richard Wins Loyalty of ◆ Rich and Poor

London, England
23 November 1193

Richard was so loved and feared that all the barons who had sided with his brother John during the Crusades now surrendered to Richard. They pledged their loyalty and protection to him alone, and in return they were given land.*

* This system of rule was called feudalism.

◆ Success ◆

Chartres, France
6 May 1194

Today is my lucky day! Many years ago I joined the guild as an apprentice, and after seven long years of working without pay, I finally became a journeyman. I learned all I could in the shop of the master of the guild. I paid my dues and abided by the rules and regulations. I saved every denier I earned, and often donated a coin or two to the needy.

And now life has rewarded me for my efforts. I have passed the final test. I just learned that my masterpiece (a carving of the head of King Philip) has been accepted by the leading members of the guild. Now I, once a poor orphan boy, will become a master in my own right. I will have my own shop and my own staff. I am going out to celebrate!

◆ Chartres in Flames ◆

Chartres, France
10 June 1194

Fire has destroyed many parts of the city of Chartres, and our beloved cathedral has been severely damaged for the second time in 50 years. We are in despair. We fear that our beloved relic, a garment worn by the Virgin Mary when she gave birth to Jesus, has been destroyed.

◆ Hope Restored ◆

Chartres, France
13 June 1194

Great cheers have gone up from the saddened population at word that our cherished relic is safe. I was standing outside the burnt-out cathedral when I saw a procession of priests carrying the relic, which survived the fire.

The cardinal made a speech declaring this was a sign from Mary that she needed a more magnificent church. I agreed and added my voice in great enthusiasm for the project. This will certainly mean more work for the carpenters' guild.

◆ Goodness Prevails ◆

Chartres, France
20 September 1194

People have gathered by the thousands in front of the cathedral praying and chanting together. Some have volunteered to drag carts filled with stones to the building site.

I have never before seen such an outpouring of love. It is said that even the bishop and the wealthy merchants and nobles are giving up part of their income for the reconstruction. These gifts have been so generous that the debris of the ruined cathedral has already been cleared, and master builders and craftsmen are setting up their workshops.

The most talented workmen in the country have come to participate in this glorious effort. I am supervising other members of the carpenters' guild as we put together wooden ramps that will make it easier to pull wagonloads of material up to the building site. There is no doubt in my mind that I am doing God's work.

◆ Circles of Comfort ◆

Chartres, France
16 March 1196

A huge round labyrinth has been set in stone on the floor of the cathedral nave. It will be used by pilgrims, who will follow the path of the labyrinth on their knees. It is believed by many that such activity brings peace to the mind and comforts the faithful.

◆ Architectural Wonders ◆

Chartres, France
17 April 1198

I have lately become friendly with the master builder who is directing the construction of the cathedral. Because he knows of my great interest in these matters, he allowed me to view his sketches, designs, and architectural plans. There is so much that is new in his vision of the cathedral that I was overwhelmed by his ideas and imagination.

His plans seem to defy gravity. The steeple will rise to incredible heights. The arches are pointed to lift the cathedral even higher.

The builder is concerned that as the walls rise up they will collapse of their own weight. However, he has come up with an amazing solution. He is planning to build bridged supports all around the outside of the cathedral to push against and buttress the thick walls. I have sketched these new "flying buttresses."

◆ Home From the Fair ◆

Chartres, France
30 July 1210

Oh, how glad I am to be back home in Chartres! I am soaking my sore and dusty feet while writing about my journey to the fair in Champagne, France. My sons had urged me to join them at the trade fair where they go each year to sell the corn and grain they raise on their farm.

Even though I had seen the feast days in Chartres, nothing prepared me for the throngs of merchants, buyers, and entertainers who came from all over the world. I was delighted to smell the aromas of spices from India and see the colors of the dyed silk from the Orient. I walked past wooden stalls piled high with leather goods from Spain, fine loomed wool from Scotland, and furs from Russia. I saw Italian bankers exchanging money and arranging loans.

There are six fairs each year, and each one lasts for almost two months. If I have the strength, I look forward to attending attending the next fair.

◆ The Magna Carta Is Signed ◆

Runneymede, England
15 June 1215

I am an old man now, and a loyal subject of King Philip of France who rules with absolute power, as kings must. So I cannot understand what has just happened in England.

King John who now sits on the English throne has just signed a document called the Magna Carta. It states "no freeman shall be taken, or imprisoned, or outlawed, or exiled, or in any way harmed . . . except by the . . . judgment of his peers or by the law of the land." When John put his seal on the Magna Carta, a law became more powerful than the King. This is unbelievable!

◆ What Will They Think of Next? ◆

Paris, France
10 May 1220

I have spoken to a friend of mine who just returned from a long sea journey. He told me that are now relying an astrolabe to measure the position of stars in the sky. He informed me that the first astrolabes were made by Arab sea men to help them find their exact location on the seas. When my friend came to France by ship, he was also amazed that the navigator used a magnetic compass that always pointed North.

THOUGHT FOR TODAY

"He who takes what is not his'n,
If he's cotched, he goes to prison."

Teaching the Middle Ages With Magnificent Art Masterpieces
Scholastic Professional Books

The Manuscripts of Modeste Ebeniste

Praise Be the Goose

Chartres, France
13 June 1220

I am particularly fond of the goose, which is a large bird that has a good brain. Moreover, they are very punctual, always returning at nightfall to their sheds.

Now the goose is certainly a tasty roasting bird, but that is not all it is good for. Goose grease never hardens, and I use it to waterproof my boots. I rub it on my chest when it is congested, and I am usually cured within the hour. The lords rub it on their armor to keep it from rusting, and the dairy maid smears it on her pots and pans to preserve their shine. I apply it over my entire body when I work outside to avoid the burn of the sun. Truth be told, I once put goose grease on my house pig to keep its skin from scorching.

Jubilation

Chartres, France
9 August 1223

Words cannot describe the beauty of the cathedral that is slowly rising from the ashes of the old. It is already the very heart of the town. All activities seem to take place around its rising walls. On feast day, cobblers, blacksmiths, secondhand clothes sellers, butchers, and bakers set up their stalls for business. Jugglers and bear tamers entertain the crowds, and monks act out plays based on the lives of the saints. I bring my family, and together we participate in the joyful happenings.

A Dream Fulfilled

Chartres, France
24 October 1260

Today our great cathedral has finally been consecrated. More than 65 years ago, I first began work on its construction. I am now a very old man, and I am overjoyed that I have lived to see this day. Thousands have come to the festivities, including every able man, woman, and child in Chartres; peasants from the surrounding countryside; visiting lords and ladies; and many important church officials. I stood with the rest of the men of the carpenters' guild under a special banner. I see my friends—the masons and blacksmiths—proudly gathered under their own colorful banners.

There was enough space in the cathedral for one and all. Those of us who were involved in its construction were bursting with pride in our accomplishments. The sun was shining through the panes of stained-glass windows, and we were all bathed in beautiful color. I knelt down and thanked God for my good fortune.

The Donor Windows From Chartres Cathedral

Dimensions: Various

Medium: Stained Glass   **Date:** Approximately 1210

• • • • • • • • • • • • • • • •

The Apothecaries and
Haberdashers
Miracles of St. Nicholas window

The Farriers
Redemption window

The Shoemakers
Assumption window

The Butchers
Miracles of Mary window

The Wheelwrights
Noah window

The Fishmongers
St. Anthony and St. Paul
the Anchorite window

The Carpenters
Noah window

The Shoemakers
Good Samaritan window

What is stained glass? ❧

Stained glass is colored glass that is flattened and cut. Eventually, like a jigsaw puzzle, the pieces are fitted into metal strips that hold the glass together and separate the colors.

Which colors were used in the stained-glass windows of Chartres? ❧

The colors were mainly the primary colors—red, blue, and yellow—plus green, white, and black. Medieval artists called these colors by the name of the precious stones they resembled. For example, red was ruby, green was emerald, and blue was called sapphire.

*Teaching the Middle Ages with Magnificent Art
Masterpieces* Scholastic Professional Books

What is a donor window? ❧

Guilds representing various groups of workmen donated money to Chartres Cathedral which was used for the construction of large stained-glass windows. These windows are called donor windows, from the word donate, or give.

Who is honored in these windows? ❧

In return for financing the windows, the contributing merchants and artisans were honored by having pictures of themselves and their crafts included.

How many occupations are honored? ❧

In the top center are farriers (blacksmiths) shoeing a horse. To prevent the horse from kicking, a workman behind the horse holds its hind leg while another workman tightly grasps the horse's bridle.

Reading the poster clockwise, the pie-shaped fragment at the top right shows a customer being fitted by a shoemaker. Directly beneath is a scene of butchers working at a trestle table, cutting up slabs of meat. Locate the customer pointing to the slice he wishes to buy.

Once again the shoemakers are honored in the bottom right-hand corner. They are shown offering a stained-glass window to the cathedral. The triangle to the left pictures two carpenters with axes in their hands, stripping the bark off a log.

Then comes a scene from the market—a fishmonger is selling his fresh catch. The bottom left corner depicts a wheelwright making a cart wheel. Lastly, the apothecary (pharmacist), with his weights balanced by a scale, is painted together with a haberdasher, who in those days sold small wares such as needles, threads, and trimmings.

Where were the donor windows placed? ❧

The donor windows were only a small part of a larger window. They were placed in the lower part of the window that could easily be seen from the ground. The windows placed closest to the public were considered the best spots. A guild felt fortunate if it was honored in the large central space, or nave, of the cathedral where most people gathered.

What was the purpose of these windows?

For the church, the biblical stories presented in the windows were used to instruct the people. Most people could neither read nor write, but they could understand the Bible stories portrayed on the windows. For a guild member, it was a way of advertising his business. A picture of a customer buying shoes might remind a worshipper that he or she needed a new pair of boots.

How did stained-glass windows change the look of medieval cathedrals?

Earlier cathedrals were dark and dreary. Small windows were fitted with wooden shutters or draped with animal skins. Architects recognized the need to enlarge windows and let in as much light as possible. Beams of light pouring through the jewel-colored windows impressed and delighted the worshippers and made the cathedral a far more hospitable place.

What is the condition of Chartres Cathedral today?

Chartres is the only medieval cathedral that has survived into the 20th century almost intact. For the past 20 years, an extensive restoration program has been ongoing to ensure that future generations will be able to appreciate its beauty and style.

Teaching the Middle Ages with Magnificent Art Masterpieces
Scholastic Professional Books

The Donor Windows From Chartres Cathedral

◆ ◆ ◆ ◆ ◆ ◆ ◆ ◆ ◆ ◆ ◆ ◆ ◆ ◆ ◆ ◆ ◆

1 **Trading Places** Workers such as masons and carpenters who learned specific crafts belonged to clubs called guilds. The guilds were responsible for training the craftsmen and looking after its members. There were guilds for road menders, bell ringers, tailors, harness makers, glass-blowers, and people who dyed cloth. Since most people couldn't read, each shop had a banner or sign illustrating its trade. Have your students identify the crafts that the following guild signs represented. Then ask them to design signs for other medieval craft guilds.

Millers

Tailors

Coopers

2 **Job Opportunities** There were many differences between work in the Middle Ages and employment today. Ask your students to compare and contrast the differences in regard to the following:

- ⚜ training
- ⚜ guilds and unions
- ⚜ employee benefits
- ⚜ salary
- ⚜ employment opportunities

3 **Come Ye to the Fair** In many ways the trade fairs in medieval times were comparable to modern shopping malls. Ask students to research European trade fairs during the 12th through 15th centuries. Then suggest that they

compile lists comparing fairs and malls by highlighting the following topics:

- ⚜ goods sold
- ⚜ food
- ⚜ money, credit, and banking
- ⚜ entertainment
- ⚜ publicity and advertising
- ⚜ diversity of countries represented

4 **Sunlit Paintings**   The stained-glass windows of Chartres Cathedral might have been the most beautiful art the people of the Middle Ages ever saw. Have students design stained-glass windows by taping colored tissue paper or colored cellophane to the sunniest windows in their classroom.

5 **A Knight to Remember**
Richard the Lionhearted was one of the most exciting knights of the Middle Ages. Tell your students to research his life and write short character sketches of one of the following:

- ⚜ Richard and his parents, Eleanor of Aquitaine and Henry II
- ⚜ Richard's allies—Frederick Barbarossa of Germany and Philip Augustus of France
- ⚜ Richard's adversaries—Saladin, leader of the Saracens; his brother John; and Duke Leopold of Austria

Invite students to share the results of their research with the class. The game Richard: Yea or Nay (pages 62–64) is a novel way to introduce students to this fascinating figure.

6 **Gothic Cathedrals**   Invite students to learn more about Chartres Cathedral and other gothic cathedrals that were built during the Middle Ages. Students might investigate how these cathedrals were built and find out more about gothic architecture. The Medieval Art and Architecture Web site (http://info.pitt.edu~medart/index.html) includes a tour of Chartres Cathedral, as well as information and photographs of other cathedrals and castles. In addition, David MacAulay's *Cathedral* (Houghton, 1981) tells the story of the construction of a gothic cathedral.

Ads on Glass

The donor windows were small parts of larger windows in the cathedral and often had interesting shapes such as triangles, circles, or quatrefoils.

In the quatrefoil below, design an appropriate symbol for either a medieval or modern craft or trade. To make your trade sign look more like a stained-glass window, you might paste colored tissue paper or colored cellophane over your design and outline the symbol with black ink.

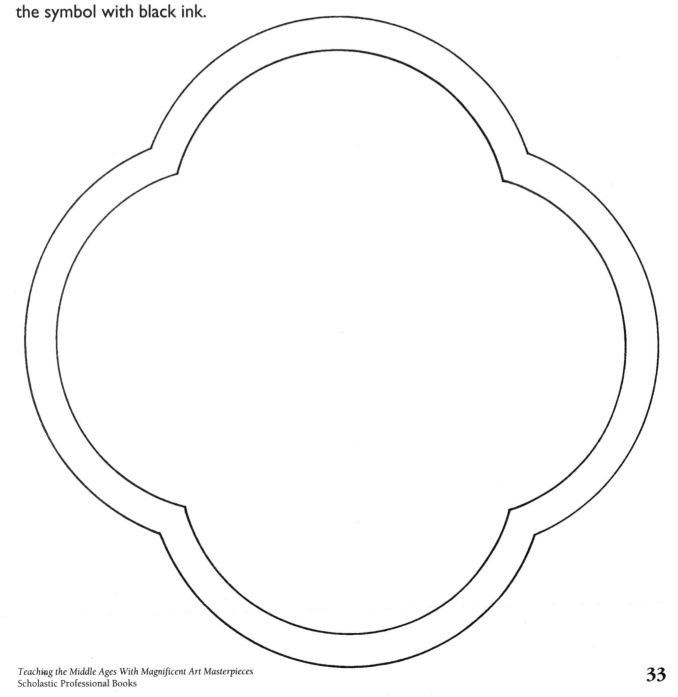

Name _____   Date _____

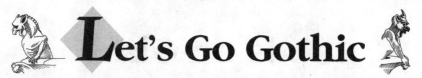

Let's Go Gothic

The architects and craftsmen of the Middle Ages introduced new ideas such as pointed arches, flying buttresses, carved doors, and stained-glass windows. These features were part of a style called Gothic.

To keep rain from pouring down on the roofs and walls of the churches, architects designed water spouts for the corners of the building. Masons made these drainpipes into fanciful stone birds or beasts called gargoyles, or "throats," that sent water shooting away from the church.

Use this outline of a medieval building to create a school, library, or sports center by adding one or more Gothic features. Place gargoyles at the corners of the roof.

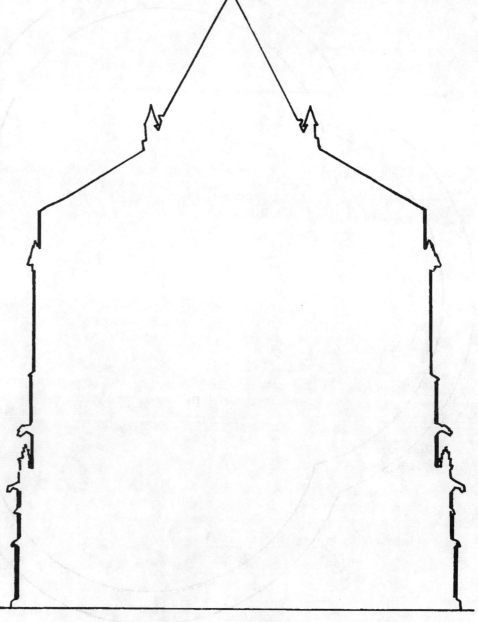

Teaching the Middle Ages With Magnificent Art Masterpieces
Scholastic Professional Books

The Life and Times
of a Scribe, Olivier Malet

Have you heard of the Duke de Berry? He is a mighty nobleman, the son and brother of kings. He is also my employer, for which I am very grateful. The Duke has a great appreciation of art and literature and will search the kingdom to get talented painters and artisans to work for him.

I have a most exciting job. I am the Duke's personal scribe and am never too far from his side. Whenever new thoughts occur to him, he dictates them to me. I copy them down on sheets of parchment made from sheepskin. The Duke has many interesting projects, and I fill up page after page. Everyone in Paris gossips about his many palaces (more than 17), collections of rare jewels, and love for beautifully illustrated books, but the Duke doesn't care. He has the power and money to do as he pleases.

Did I ever tell you how I first met such an illustrious personage? My father was a professional scribe who copied books to be used by scholars at the nearby University of Paris. These books were called *manuscripts* because they were written by hand. His small workshop employed only two other copyists—and me, as soon as I was old enough to write. The workshop was never heated because a fire might ignite all the carefully written pages.

Can you imagine our astonishment when one winter's day the Duke entered our humble room? He was accompanied by seven servants, his personal chaplain, and three bodyguards. There was hardly enough space to move, yet I remember my father trying to bow in front of this great lord. As a result of this visit, my father was commissioned to do the calligraphy for a small prayer book. Oh, we rejoiced that night, and Mother roasted a goose, which was a rare treat for us.

By the way, as soon as I learned to write, Papa insisted that I keep a diary, which I hope you will take the time to read.

◆ ◆ ◆ ◆ ◆ ◆ ◆ ◆ ◆ ◆ ◆ ◆ ◆ ◆ ◆ ◆

DISCUSSION QUESTION: During the Middle Ages, communication was limited to conversation and handwritten manuscripts. What types of rapid communication are available to us today? How have these new technologies changed our lives?

The Diaries of Olivier Malet

◆ Ship of Dread ◆

Paris, France
7 November 1347

I heard my parents whispering last night. I could tell by their hushed voices and sad expression that something terrible was going on. I must confess that I listened to their conversation without permission, and what I heard frightened me enormously. They spoke of a merchant ship carrying many sick and dying passengers that docked at the port of Marseille in southern France. A few crew members actually came ashore before the ship was ordered to depart at once. They fear the ship carries the plague.

◆ The Black Death ◆

Paris, France
17 July 1348

The Black Death is upon us! Those who could afford to leave have abandoned Paris and the country. Mother does not let me out of the house.

No one knows where the plague originated, but most say it comes from vapors in the atmosphere. I have even wondered if it could possibly be spread by infected rats and the fleas that live on them.

It is said that so many bodies are being brought to the churches each day that the burial grounds cannot hold them. The city seems empty and silent except for the church bells tolling for the dead. Rumors are spreading that the wife of our King

John II has died of the sickness. Nobody is safe! Can it be true that one half the population of Paris has died?

◆ Doctors in Disguise ◆

Paris, France
10 September 1348

Doctors making house calls are seen in the streets of Paris wearing birdlike masks. The beaks are filled with herbs and medicine to protect them from poisonous vapors.

◆ Ring-Around-the-Rosy ◆

Paris, France
1 October 1348

I hear the children outside singing a song that I have learned was started by the English during the dreadful Black Death. These children, full of life and high spirits, have no idea how gruesome this little song really is.

Teaching the Middle Ages With Magnificent Art Masterpieces
Scholastic Professional Books

The plague often causes a hideous, round, rose-colored-rash—"ring around the rosy." The disease is accompanied by a horrible smell so people sometimes carry flowers—"a pocket full of posey"—to mask the odor. Often the bodies have to be burned to prevent the further spread of infection—"ashes, ashes, all fall down" really doesn't need any explanation. I hope these youngsters never learn the real meaning of their innocent game.

◆ Surviving the Devastation ◆

Paris, France
Spring 1349

We have survived, but hundreds of thousands have not been so lucky. The whole country is in shock. How could this happen? Will the plague return?

The Great Dying has created an immense labor shortage. There are areas where entire villages of peasants were wiped out. There is no one left to till the fields or milk the cows or plant the corn. Rather than see their land ruined, the nobles are making desperate efforts to get workers. They are even offering peasants wages for their services. This has never before happened. Our traditional way of life is changing.

◆ France and England at War ◆

Paris, France
12 June 1356

Will France's suffering never end? As long as I can remember our country has been at war with England.* The English king controls huge areas of French land, and battle after battle takes place, men die, taxes are raised, peace treaties are signed, but there is never a solution to the problem. Now word has reached Paris that King John and many important nobles, including his 16-year-old son the Duke de Berry, have been taken hostage on the battlefield and are being held for ransom in England.

* Hundred Years' War

◆ A Country in Chaos ◆

Paris, France
Spring 1358

Can I not write something pleasant in this diary? With the King held prisoner in England the country is in chaos. Large bands of lawless highwaymen called routiers are terrorizing the peasants and country folk. Many suspect that they are English who have crossed the Channel to make trouble. They capture villages, kill the inhabitants, rob and plunder and burn the land. We who live in Paris are afraid to travel beyond the city walls.

◆ French Peasants Revolt ◆

Rouen, France
22 July 1358

The peasants in the country have risen up against their landlords. They are killing the nobles and burning their castles. Perhaps they are trying to get even for centuries of abuse.

❧ The Diaries of Olivier Malet ❧

The peasants are furious because the routiers, lawless highwaymen, were allowed to rob and terrorize them, and no knight protected them. They are also angry at the tax collectors who take their money and give it to lords living in palaces. I guess the last straw was the demand of many lords who were taken prisoner by the English. They wanted the peasants to contribute money for their release.

Can anyone blame them for wishing for revenge? But many peace-loving people are wondering when all this horror will end.

◆ King John Is Dead: ◆ Long Live King Charles V

Paris, France
12 October 1364

King John died in England, still a captive, at the age of 45, after a short illness. His son Charles V, the brother of the Duke de Berry, has ascended to the throne. Though he is neither strong nor handsome, Charles is a man of great intellect and a very able leader. France has great need of his wisdom in these troubled times.

Those of us who have glimpsed the King fear for his health. He often takes to his bed with an overwhelming physical weakness. Charles may not be a man of action, but he has the same taste for luxury as his brother the Duke de Berry, who still remains a captive in London.

◆ The Duke de Berry is Ransomed ◆

Paris, France
19 April, 1367

The ransom has been paid and the Duke de Berry has returned to France. When he is not involved in matters of war and diplomacy, he is pursuing his interest in the arts.

◆ Rules for a Scribe ◆

How to Make Parchment

I. Remove the skin of a sheep and soak it in lime.

II. Wash it over and over.

III. Stretch it on a frame to dry.

IV. Rub it with a pumice stone until it is thin and smooth.

V. Cut it to the proper size.

VI. Mark off your margins and draw lines across each page as a guide for lettering. Be sure to leave space for illuminated letters.

VII. Make ink from soot mixed with gum and acid.

VIII. The best pens are made from goose quills or reeds. Remember to work slowly and with great patience!

Teaching the Middle Ages With Magnificent Art Masterpieces
Scholastic Professional Books

❖ A Woman Is Chosen to ❖ Illuminate the Duke's Manuscripts

Paris, France
12 May 1368

I hear that the Duke de Berry has hired Jeanne de Montbaston to illuminate one of his books. It is quite an honor for a woman. Jeanne, who is very accomplished in her craft, was trained by her father.

❖ The Louvre Becomes a ❖ Beautiful Palace

Paris, France
June 1367

Charles V commissioned his master mason, Raymond du Temple, to make the Louvre fortress into a fashionable and livable palace. One of the notable additions was hot baths with adjoining warming rooms, a vogue that was encouraged by a growing interest in the ancient Roman baths.

The grounds surrounding the palace have numerous orchards and gardens where the invited nobility delight in Charles's menagerie of birds, boars, dromedaries, nightingales, and lions. I was lucky enough to be introduced to Guy Martin, a young man who was recently given the post of Keeper of the King's Wild Beasts.

There is no doubt that chief among the King's treasures is his library of more than 900 manuscripts, which are kept in a tower close to the royal quarters. This richly decorated library is probably unequaled in all of Europe.

NEWS FROM ABROAD
❖ Marco Polo Travels to Cathay* ❖

Venice, Italy
5 May 1380

The Duke has not stopped talking about a travel diary written by a Venetian merchant named Marco Polo, who traveled over land to Asia from 1274 to 1279. Marco Polo described the splendor in which the ruler Kublai Khan lived. He also wrote that the ports of Cathay were the busiest in the world, shipping silks, spices, and lustrous porcelain throughout the East.

* China

✦ Lead Into Gold ✦

Paris, France
6 February 1391

We have all heard of these dedicated individuals who spend their lives hidden in secret laboratories while they search to discover the nature of all things. Many of them are obsessed with the quest to turn ordinary metal into gold. These alchemists, as they are called, are often condemned as evil magicians and sometimes live in terrible poverty.

✦ Chaucer Takes a Daring Gamble ✦

London, England
12 December 1400

The Duke told me that an English fellow named Geoffrey Chaucer has just died. Men of letters are talking about a collection of stories he had been writing called "The Canterbury Tales."

The collection is about a group of pilgrims traveling to a shrine who amuse each other by telling stories. The tales are said to be funny, lively, and clever, but Chaucer did a shocking thing. Instead of writing in Latin as every literate person does, he actually wrote in the common language of English. I wonder if anyone will ever read it . . .

✦ What Will They Think of Next? ✦

Paris, France
30 April 1401

Growing more and more popular are a variety of inventions that the Duke and his friends are using every day.

Spectacles, glass lenses said to improve eyesight, are enabling the Duke to continue to use his vast library though his vision is failing in old age. The glasses are fastened to handles usually made of leather. Of course, the Duke's frames are gold.

Instead of listening for the church bell that rings at prayer to determine time, the Duke now depends upon a mechanical clock.

Très Riches Heures, October

Dimensions: 8¹/₄ inches x 11¹/₂ inches

Medium: Ink and paint on vellum   **Date:** Approximately 1416

• • • • • • • • • • • • • • • •

What clues in the painting indicate the month of October? ❧

Golden leaves on the trees and foliage mark the season. In the fall fields were planted with wheat, rye, or some other grain. *October* is also the title of this painting, which is one page of a very famous illuminated manuscript called *Très Riches Heures*.

What is an illuminated manuscript? ❧

An illuminated manuscript is a hand-painted work of art found in a handwritten book. A painting like *October* is called a miniature, not because it is small, but because red ink is often used in the calligraphy. In Latin, the written language used during the Middle Ages, *miniatus* means "colored with red." Therefore the word miniature in the illuminated manuscripts refers to the color rather than the size.

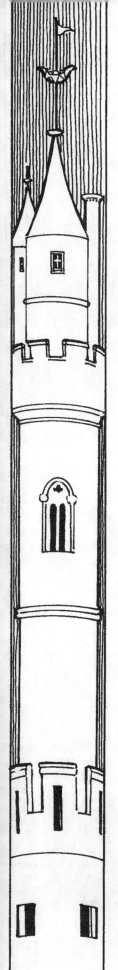

What was the purpose of these illuminated manuscripts?

During the Middle Ages, personal prayer books called Books of Hours were very popular. They were carefully painted and written by hand by talented artists and scribes. Sometimes the first part of a Book of Hours was a calendar that illustrated an event appropriate to each month of the year. These books were generally commissioned by well-to-do patrons. A calendar appears at the top of the painting *October*.

Who commissioned "Très Riches Heures"?

The Duke de Berry commissioned the work. He was not only a patron of the arts, but a man of enlightened taste. His particular passion was beautiful books, and he enjoyed encouraging exceptional artists.

Who were the artists who painted this book?

To illustrate the manuscript, the Duke called upon the talents of the three Limbourg brothers: Paul, Herman, and Jean. Paul, the eldest and most gifted, is thought to be responsible for this particular miniature. While many Books of Hours are restricted to religious subjects, the calendar in *Très Riches Heures* illustrates the personal life of the Duke. His palaces figure very prominently in many of the miniatures, and his face is depicted in one of the paintings. These paintings allow us to peek into life in the 14th century.

What made the style of the Limbourg brothers so unique?

The Limbourgs were the first to pay detailed attention to landscape painting. They were keen observers and were thought to paint while using a magnifying glass. This miniature is also unique because it is the first known painting in Western art to utilize reflections and shadows.

What reflections and shadows can you find in the painting?

Shadows are cast on the ground, and people and boats are reflected in the water. One man's shadow is seen on the palace wall. From the position of the shadows, it may be early afternoon.

Where do you think the artist was standing when he painted this miniature?

One of the Duke de Berry's many residences was directly across the Seine River from the Louvre. The painting was done from the upper window of this residence, looking out and down.

Teaching the Middle Ages With Magnificent Art Masterpieces
Scholastic Professional Books

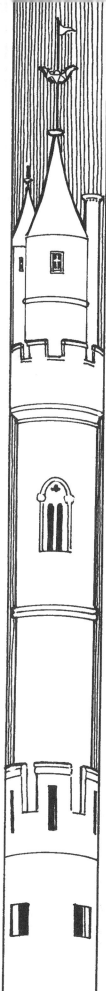

How does the artist draw our eyes into the distance? ❧

He uses a series of diagonal lines. A diagonal line of greenery begins at the left edge of the field and is augmented by the diagonals in the plow (harrow) and in the steps. He also used bold colors in the foreground, which are repeated in diminishing scale in the background.

Since they didn't have paper in the 14th century, what material did the artist use to create this miniature? ❧

It was painted on 206 bound sheets of fine vellum, a parchment made of sheep-skin or calfskin.

How did the Limbourgs acquire their paints? ❧

The colors they used were prepared in their workshop from minerals, plants, and chemicals. Violet came from sunflowers; black came from soot or ground charcoal. Some of the minerals the artists used, like gold powder or the blue stone lapis lazuli, were so precious they were kept in leather bags in the Duke's apartments.

Did any other artists work on "Très Riches Heures"? ❧

In 1416 the three Limbourg brothers died, as did the Duke de Berry. These simultaneous deaths led to the conclusion that they all died of a sudden outbreak of the plague. At their deaths, the book was not yet completed, and was finished at a later date by another artist.

How would you describe the building that dominates the background? ❧

It is a large, white, multi-turreted stone palace called the Louvre. In this painting it appears to be a castle straight out of a children's fairy tale. However, it didn't always look this way. Originally built in 1190 as a fortress tower, it was a dark and gloomy citadel. The Louvre was used as a storage room for the King's treasures as well as a prison for his enemies.

Can you guess the purpose of the outer wall? ❧

The wall that encircles the palace was built to provide added protection. Balconies project out of the top of the wall. Openings were cut into the floor of the balconies through which stones or boiling liquids could be dropped on attackers. The walls also had guard towers and tooth-shaped indentations with gaps between them called battlements. They enabled the defenders to fire while still remaining behind cover. However, the walls of the Louvre were never used for defensive purposes.

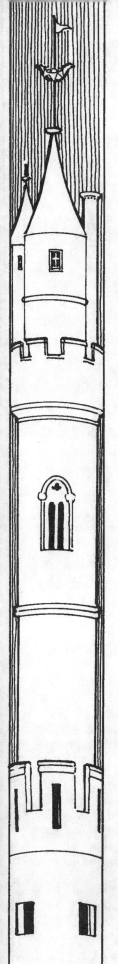

What is the Louvre used for today? ⟨⟨⟩

The Louvre is one of the greatest art museums in the world.

How many people can be seen strolling along the left bank of the Seine River? ⟨⟨⟩

Ten well-dressed city folk are walking, and one person is pictured coming through the back gate. Perhaps he has just seen the King.

What activities are taking place in the river? ⟨⟨⟩

At the bottom of one set of steps, women are washing clothes by beating them with sticks; at the other set of steps are three boats, one of which is occupied, possibly by a fisherman.

Almost in the center of the painting is the strange figure of an archer. What is his purpose? ⟨⟨⟩

With humor, the Limbourgs have painted a scarecrow with a bow and arrow, ready to protect his fields from the intruding crows. The white strips of cloth blowing in the breeze assist the scarecrow in keeping the birds away.

What does the large figure in blue on the right appear to be doing? ⟨⟨⟩

He is a peasant sowing seeds that he carries in a white pouch. The expression on his face seems to reflect the boredom of this repetitive task. In the foreground lies a white bag filled with grain and an object with a long strap that might be a carrying case.

What is the peasant on horseback pulling? ⟨⟨⟩

He is pulling a harrow, a heavy piece of farm equipment with sharp upright teeth on the underside. It was used to break up and level the plowed ground. The heavy stone on the harrow will push the teeth of the plow more deeply into the soil.

How did lifestyle of the peasants differ from the lifestyle of the nobility? ⟨⟨⟩

The Louvre was the home of kings and queens, lords, and ladies. This nobility lived within the palace with wealth and privilege as their birthright. In contrast, the peasants in the foreground had to receive permission to settle on the lord's land and had to work part of the time for the lord or give him rent or a share of the crops.

Teaching the Middle Ages With Magnificent Art Masterpieces
Scholastic Professional Books

Très Riches Heures, October

. . . .

1 **Crime and Punishment During the Middle Ages** Laws were often unfair, and punishments were usually extremely harsh during the Middle Ages. The following is a case that might have occurred in medieval times.

> *Farmer Odbold claims that he was walking to the market when Squire Radulf's horse was stung by a bee. The horse violently kicked Odbold, knocking him to the ground. However, Radulf charges that the farmer intentionally poked the horse in the rear with his staff, causing the horse to kick.*

> *A meeting was held and all agreed that Radulf's guilt will be determined by the ordeal of the hot iron. Radulf will be made to carry three pounds of hot iron for 15 feet. Then his hand will be bandaged, and if after three days, it seems to be healing, he will be declared innocent of all charges.*

Ask your class to discuss the case. What other factors should determine the guilt or innocence of the accused? What would be their verdict? If Radulf is found guilty, what punishment do they suggest?

2 **Sealed for Safety** Scribes were given the task of writing letters or important documents for kings and nobles. Since even nobility often could not write their names, they used seals instead of signatures. The wax stamp or seal also proved that the letter was not a forgery. Have your students design their personal seal using clay.

3 **Author, Author** Until the 12th century, church officials and educated people used Latin for writing manuscripts, books, and poetry. From about 1150, however, some authors began to write in the vernacular—the language spoken by the people in their own country or region. Dante Alighieri wrote in Italian and Geoffrey Chaucer wrote in English. Ask students to research these famous authors

and tell about their poems and stories. Students might also want to read selections from *The Canterbury Tales*. Adaptations of this classic are available for young readers, including *The Canterbury Tales* by Geoffrey Chaucer and Geraldine McCaughrean (Puffin, 1997).

4 **Recalling Camelot** Many legends exist about knights in shining armor. Perhaps the most famous is the story of King Arthur and the Knights of the Round Table who lived in Camelot. Have students research this story and get to know the characters of King Arthur, Merlin, Lancelot, and the beautiful Queen Guinevere. Then ask them to make up their own legends about special places in days of old and the characters who lived and fought there. Suggest that students create plays about their characters, and act them out.

5 **Medieval Math** Ask students to solve the following medieval math problems. Have them write their answers in Roman numerals.

❧ A monk named Bede who lived 673 A.D. to 735 A.D. wrote about 80 books by hand. He completed about 3 books per year. About how many years did it take Bede to write the books?

❧ A messenger was sent from Chartres to Avignon, a distance of 400 miles, to tell the Pope that his presence was wanted for the dedication of Chartres Cathedral. The messenger had to return to Chartres to give the Pope's reply. If a horse and rider traveled 15 miles per hour, how many days would it take a messenger to make this round-trip journey? Remember—messengers traveled in daylight, only 12 hours a day (about 4½ days).

   Then challenge students to write their own medieval math problems. They can write their problems on index cards and then exchange problems with other class members.

Teaching the Middle Ages With Magnificent Art Masterpieces
Scholastic Professional Books

Illuminate a Letter

In the illuminated manuscript *Très Riches Heure,* the first capital letter of each chapter is elaborately decorated with leaves and flowers drawn around the letter. Using the first letter of your name, or a letter of your choice, design your own illuminated letter and decoration in the manner of the scribes of medieval days.

Create a Calendar

The artists of the Middle Ages included calendars in their Books of Hours. Select a month that has special meaning to you. In the space below, draw a picture that best depicts that particular month.

In medieval times, the birthdays of special people such as St. Valentine and St. Patrick were written in red letters. From that time on, an important holiday became known as a "red-letter" day. Number the the days of the month, including your red-letter days.

Sunday	Monday	Tuesday	Wednesday	Thursday	Friday	Saturday

Teaching the Middle Ages With Magnificent Art Masterpieces
Scholastic Professional Books

The Life and Times
of a Duchess, Germaine de Valery

 I was born into the highest ranks of the nobility and always knew that the blood of the kings of France flowed through my veins.

I was betrothed to be married to Duke Hebert when he was 11 and I was just 6 years old. Our parents thought it would be advantageous to both families if our fortunes and land could be joined. Neither Hebert nor I had any say in the matter. Arranged marriages are very common—I have never met anyone who married for love.

From the time of my betrothal until my wedding nine years later, my days were spent preparing to be a good wife and a successful hostess. I learned how to read and write, sing, play the lute and harp, ride well, and do fine needlework. I became expert at chess and the art of conversation, and could even recognize which herbs could heal the sick. In other words, I was getting ready for my role as a lady of the manor.

After my marriage I realized that I would frequently be alone. Duke Hebert was often called away from the castle on government business or to inspect his other properties. On more than one occasion his squire readied his armor and together they left to fight a war. Naturally, I was well trained to take over his duties and see to the welfare of all the people who lived in the keep.*

But my primary responsibility was to care for my two children, Marguerite and Henri. Until they reached the age of seven, I personally supervised their education. Then Henri became a page, the first step on his journey to knighthood. Marguerite was sent to the nuns' convent for her education until she was 16. Now, to my joy, she is to be married. Auguste Poitiers has asked for Marguerite's hand. I have recorded the exciting events of this time in my memoirs.

* within the castle walls

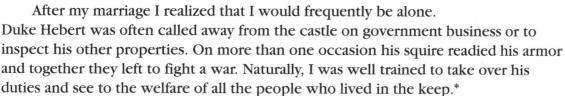

DISCUSSION QUESTION: In the Middle Ages women were often limited by attitudes and customs of the times. Scholars are discovering, however, that medieval women were not only wives and mothers, but in some cases healers, artists, religious leaders, managers, writers, and thinkers. How has the role of women changed in modern times? What women have made major contributions to society?

The Memoirs of Germaine de Valery

✦ Marguerite's Dowry ✦ Is Settled

Eze, France
2 June 1448

I have waited many years for Marguerite's wedding day to arrive. Finally, after days of negotiations, the financial settlement between the two families has been agreed upon. The bride's dowry will consist of several parcels of valuable land and a large sum of money.

Marguerite was much sought after since she is an heiress with a large fortune. I have instructed my husband, Duke Hebert, to make sure that Marguerite's rights are protected. French laws don't guard the rights of women.

✦ We Will Host a ✦ Tournament

Eze, France
12 July 1448

So many decisions to make each day! Duke Hebert is rarely available for consultation because he is busy training his new falcon.

After days of deliberation we are to celebrate the marriage by hosting a tournament that will take place following the wedding.

✦ Thank You, Duke Rene ✦

Eze, France
8 August 1448

I have just acquired a splendid book written by Duke Rene of Anjou, who knows everything there is to know about the right way to run a tournament. I have spent hours reading the *Treatise on the Form and Devising of a Tournament*, and I have made pages of notes on the proper procedures, from the opening day to the concluding ceremonies.

✦ The Date Is Set ✦

Eze, France
5 September 1448

I have decided that early May will be the best time for the outdoor event to take place. We hope the weather will be favorable for travel. I trust that the day will still be cool enough for the knights to wear their armor in comfort. I once went to a tournament where many knights fainted from the heat. Certainly I do not want this to happen at any party for which I am responsible.

Also, scheduling so far in advance should give ample time for my heralds and their trumpeters to travel to even the furthest destination to deliver the invitations. These will be addressed to all men who can prove their knighthood. The heralds will announce the time and place of the tournament, how the knights' performances will be judged, and what prizes will be available to the winners. Of course, invitations will also go out to all our dear friends and family as well as the Duke of Anjou, who often participates in such events. I expect between 900 and 1,000 guests, and almost as many servants, to join us for the festivities.

◆ Sew and Sew ◆

Eze, France
22 October 1448

I have summoned the best seamstresses to design the outfits Marguerite and I will wear. Marguerite selected (with my advice, of course) a pale-blue silk embroidered with gold and silver threads and trimmed with fur. As is the custom, the neckline will be low and the waistline high.

I am very pleased with my choice of a dark-blue velvet trimmed with row upon row of silk flowers.

My biggest problem is what to wear on my head. I have been having daily discussions with my milliner, and we have decided that a red hennin, the towering cone headdress draped with veils, will be most appropriate. Marguerite will wear a taller version of this most popular style in white.

◆ Building the Battlefield ◆

Eze, France
1 March 1449

Duke Hebert is supervising the building of the lists, a stout double fence in the south meadow of our estate. It must be made of strong timber to contain the battle. We must also construct observers' stands. My household staff is making sure there is enough room in the castle for the most important guests. All others will be housed in tents on the border of the south meadow.

◆ Banquet Banter ◆

Eze, France
12 March 1449

I seem to spend more time with the cooks and bakers than with my peers. Talks are endless about how to prepare and serve food to so many guests. It is expected that we will have the usual ten courses. The menu for each day of the festivities must vary, of course, and the Duke and I would be shamed if anyone left the table hungry.

Everybody's nerves are on edge. Yesterday the head cook threw a temper tantrum. He says he needs more help in the kitchen. I will have to use the young pages to assist my servants in acting as waiters.

I am so pleased with the menu for the wedding feast that I am preserving it in my memoir.

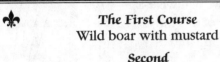

The First Course
Wild boar with mustard

Second
Venison served with milk, sugar, and wheat

Third
Roast bear on spit

Fourth
Pigeon pie, Eel pie

Fifth
Baked porpoise

Sixth
Lobster, shrimp, and crayfish

Seventh
Pork en croute, decorated with four angels

Eighth
Succulent swan

Ninth
A special confection in the shape
of a bride and groom

Finale
24 live blackbirds baked in a pie

✦ A Procession of Guests ✦

Eze, France
30 April 1449

The ceremonies will not begin for another four days, but as I look down the road, I can see lines of horsemen and horsewomen making their way to the castle. Our guests are beginning to arrive. They are accompanied by their squires and pages bearing brightly colored banners and shields. Everyone from the castle has come out to witness the colorful procession.

I am overjoyed with the spectacle, but can't stop thinking that every new arrival must be fed  and housed and every horse must be stabled. I smile. Our noble family of Valery will do it in style.

✦ At Last! ✦

Eze, France
Morning, 5 May 1449

Today is the wedding day. Many of our friends and family will walk together to the parish church in the village where my cousin the bishop will conduct the service. We are led by the musicians with their flutes, harps, and viols. Next is Marguerite, riding on a black mule whose harness is of gold and scarlet. Hebert has the honor of swinging his beautiful daughter up into the saddle and proudly leads the mule along the path. Her fiancé, Auguste follows on a white horse, escorted by gaily dressed squires and all the noble guests.

No work is being done by the villagers today. They line the road cheering as the wedding party sweeps past. The bishop meets them at the door of the church and it is here that they exchange vows. Now Marguerite and her groom scatter new silver coins to the swarms of people elbowing to get close to the marvelous pair. Finally, the church door is thrown open and all the guests are seated for a mass. Hundreds of candles burn, and the stained-glass windows reflect the light like jewels.

❖ The Festivities Commence ❖

Eze, France
Afternoon, 5 May 1449

We all return to the great hall of the castle, which is decorated with tapestries and yards and yards of red and green silk. Fresh flowers are scattered on the floor. Then Hebert, as the host, presents suitable gifts to each of the guests.

Soon the trumpets sound announcing that the reception is over and the wedding banquet is about to begin. I have planned for the bridal party to dine in a tent of pink silk. The remainder of the guests will sit at long tables in the glorious sunshine. The food is served, the troubadours tell tales, the jugglers entertain, and I have never been so happy.

❖ Time for the Tourney ❖

Eze, France
Evening, 5 May 1449

It is time to start the preparations for the tournament which will begin tomorrow morning. It is a tradition for the competing knights to take part in a ceremony where they exhibit their helmets in front of the noble ladies and judges. It is the duty of the noble ladies and judges to point out those knights guilty of unchivalrous conduct.

If a knight has broken his word, acted in cowardice, or is known to have mistreated or insulted a woman, he is considered unworthy and is forbidden to take part in the tournament. Fortunately, all our knights passed the test and can look forward to days of glory.

For me, the most exciting part was to see my dear son, Henri, who has just recently attained knighthood, participate in this ceremony. Tomorrow he will take part in his first tournament. I bless him and pray for his safety.

❖ Henri Wins First Prize ❖

Eze, France
10 May 1449

My son, Henri, stunned us all by unseating seven knights and taking first prize in the tournament. The prize of a bear was presented to him by one of the most famous and accomplished ladies, Christine of Pizan. She composed this poem, and a troubadour set it to music:

In this gracious month of May,
When flowers bloom and birds delight,
Henri of Valery became a knight
So in a tourney, he might play.
Honor he brings to the name of Valery,
He broke five lances, so steady his aim,
We, spectators, went wild with acclaim,
He has won our hearts, the brave Henri.

Henri shyly told me that months of practicing with his squire at the quintain* had helped build his muscles and improve his aim.

* Used for practice only, a quintain was a swiveling wooden device mounted on a pole. On one side was a dummy knight with a shield.

DID YOU KNOW?

Since fashion has become so important, every lady wants cloth woven from natural white wool. Therefore, darker wools are not highly valued. Shepherds call their worthless flock "black sheep."

A new white silk made in Constantinople is called diaper, from the Greek word *diapros*, which means "pure white." Now any white cloth is called diaper, whether it is used for table linens or swaddling babies.

❧ What's the Point? ❧

Eze, France
15 October 1450

What nonsense! The long pointed toes of men's shoes prevent all physical exercise and have resulted in many broken legs and ankles. I have heard of one silly fellow who chained the points of his shoe to his knee!

Duke Hebert told me that some French knights actually cut off the points of their shoes when they had to jump down from their horses to run from their enemies. Hebert assured me that he would never wear such a ridiculous style.

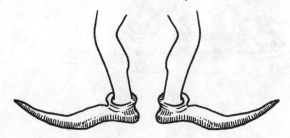

❧ Dangerous Beauty ❧

Eze, France
23 April 1451

What can I say about current women's fashions? Lately, my friends and I are wearing starched veils which are supported and raised by long lengths of wire and held in place by countless numbers of pins. It is rumored that the Queen of France bought 8,900 English pins for her head!

GOOD MANNERS FOR GIRLS

My friend Jean Sulpice wrote these tips for proper young ladies.

- ◆ Your tongue should not be covered with filth.

- ◆ Make sure no drippings hang from your nose like icicles.

- ◆ Comb your hair. Do not stuff your head-dress with feathers and trash.

- ◆ Do not remove neck fleas and then kill them in front of others.

The Tournament

Medium: Ink and paint on vellum   **Date:** Approximately 1455–1460

• • • • • • • • • • • • • • • • • •

What do you think is happening in this scene? ✦

Groups of knights on horseback are competing in a tournament. A tournament resembles a battle, but it is really a showcase for the knights to fight each other with only a moderate risk of serious injury or death. The knights in this scene are carrying blunt-tipped swords. This illustration is referred to as *The Mêlèe with Swords*. A mêlèe was a tournament in which two teams of knights meet as if on a battlefield. These differed from jousts, in which individual knights fought each other.

What was the purpose of a tournament? ✦

Originally, tournaments were a way for a knight to practice real warfare. Groups of knights would face each other in an open field where there were no rules and many injuries or deaths. When gunpowder became widely available in the 15th century, the knight and his armor became obsolete, and tournaments became celebrations hosted by very wealthy nobility and, on occasion, the king himself.

Where did a tournament take place? ✦

A tournament was usually held on a level field outside the castle walls. A double row of wooden rails mark off the oblong shape called "the lists." It is within the lists that the tournament took place. Any knight who ventured outside the lists would be disqualified. Locate the lists in the illustration.

Why were so many knights willing to participate in such a dangerous pastime? ❧

It was a way for a knight to gain personal fame and to attract the admiration of the ladies. It was also a way for knights to get very rich since the loser would have to give up his horse, harness, and armor to the winner. Often the victors were rewarded with prizes of great value.

How were the knights dressed? ❧

A knight wore a sleeveless coat of armor called a cuirass, which was pierced with holes to make it weigh less. Their armguards were either made of metal or treated leather, and they carried shields emblazoned with their coats of arms. A knight's head was covered with a leather tournament cap that had an iron spike on top designed to hold the knight's crest. The crest is the large object, often fantastically decorated, that sits on top of the helmet. Locate the red stag crest and the man's head crest to the left of the center in the illustration. Look for other interesting crests.

What advantage did a cuirass have over the complete iron suit? ❧

The cuirass was much lighter, weighing only about 55 pounds. A full suit or armor could weigh 150 to 200 pounds, as much as the knight himself.

Why did a knight need to have a coat of arms? ❧

In the 12th century, knights began wearing helmets that completely concealed their faces except for two narrow slits for the eyes. It made a knight unrecognizable to both his friends and his enemies. Symbols such as lions or other beasts were painted on the knights' shields and banners to aid in recognition during a battle. As time went on these decorations were repeated on the surcoat (a sleeveless garment that was worn over armor)—therefore the name, coat of arms. By the 15th century, as the designs became more complex, it developed into a complicated science called heraldry—a system of personal symbols by which a knight could be recognized.

Which two coat of arms can you find repeated in several places in the painting? ❧

The coat of arms on the blue banner—a gold fleur-de-lis with a red stripe—on the left side of the painting and the coat of arms on the tan banner in the center of the painting are repeated in many places. Both appear on the judges stand, on the banners on the right side of the painting, and on the trumpeters' banners.

Where else in the painting are coats of arms displayed?

Locate the coats of arms that identify the tournament judges in the booth in the left corner. It is their job to declare the winners or disqualify a knight who fights unfairly. Also, on the right are squires holding banners with their lord's coat of arms.

What was the function of these squires?

A squire was a young man of noble blood who was training for the knighthood. It was the next step after serving as a page. There were very specific duties for a squire. At a tournament he dressed his lord and carried his arms before the fight. If his lord were thrown from his horse, the squire would help him back up and rearm him.

Who is seated in the red box to the right of the judges stand?

These elegantly dressed noble ladies have a box seat with a clear view of the action. Each one probably has selected the knight who she hopes will cover himself with glory. In her excitement, the lady might cheer or call out to her knight, or fling off her veil or remove a ribbon from her dress and throw it at her favorite knight.

How did a knight win at a tournament?

The tournament was governed by rules of conduct that specified that the taking of prisoners was the object of the game. There was also a point designation. A knight received points for unseating another knight, striking his opponent's visor three times, or breaking the most lances. The team who captured the most prisoners and had the greatest number of points would win. A knight could be disqualified for striking an opponent who had his back turned or hitting an opponent below the waist. The team who captured the most prisoners and had the greatest number of points would win. In this tournament, most knights carried blunt-tipped swords, though some fought with wooden maces and light wooden lances with dull tips.

Which artist created this painting?

This painting is part of Duke Rene of Anjou's book, *Treatise on the Form and Devising of a Tournament*, which was a medieval "how-to" book on the etiquette of tournaments. Anjou was known to be a gifted artist, and the paintings in the book are often attributed to him. He had a very interesting life and ruled briefly as the King of Naples.

How does the artist's use of color enhance the painting?

Primary colors are repeated throughout the painting, adding visual excitement. The knights fighting in the tournament are in yellow, blue, and red, colors which also appear on the banners on the right side of the painting.

The Tournament

1 **A Knightly Code** The following is a Code of Honor that knights tried to follow.

I. Let a strong religious belief guide your life.

II. Obey those to whom you have sworn allegiance.

III. Show kindness and compassion to those weaker than you.

IV. Love your country.

V. Display steadfast courage when facing the enemy.

VI. Show courtesy and respect toward women.

VII. Never break your word or tell a lie.

VIII. Give generously to those in need.

IX. Be a leader who sets a good example.

Discuss with your class which of these rules of behavior are still important today. Is there a rule that no longer applies? What rules might you add? Have your class create a modern code of behavior.

2 **A Time for Rhyme** During the Middle Ages, minstrels, troubadours, knights, and ladies wrote and sang poems about love. They also told stories in poems called ballads. Each ballad was made up of a series of dramatic scenes which led to a tragic or triumphant ending. Here is part of an old ballad called "Sir Patrick Spens."

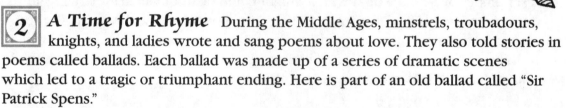

The king sits in Dumferling town,
Drinking the blood-red wine:
"O where will I get a good sailor,
To sail this ship of mine."

Up and spoke an elder knight,
Sat at the king's right knee,
"Sir Patrick Spens is the best sailor,
That sails upon the sea."

The king has written a broad letter,
And signed it with his hand,
And sent it to Sir Patrick Spens,
Who was walking on the sand.

The first line that Sir Patrick read,
A loud laugh, laughed he,
The next line that Sir Patrick read,
The tear blinded his eye.

"O who is this has done this deed,
This ill deed done to me,
To send me out this time o' the year,
To sail upon the sea!

"Make haste, make haste, my merry men all,
Our good ship sails the morn:"
"O say not so, my master dear,
For I fear a deadly storm."

What do students think happened to Sir Patrick Spens? Have your class finish this ballad or write one of their own. Remind them that a ballad can retell a story or an historic event. Provide a copy of the ballad "Sir Patrick Spens," or challenge students to find a copy of it.

3 ***Women of Valor*** Several women of medieval times made contributions to history and changed the world in which they lived. A few notable women include Lady Margaret Beaufort, who founded Christ's and St. John's Colleges at Cambridge; Joan of Arc, who as a soldier forced the English out of France; and Christine de Pisan, who wrote poems and books celebrating the morality and intelligence of women at a time when they were not highly regarded. Have your students research these outstanding women and others of the time, and write brief biographies of their lives.

4 ***Food Fit for a King***
The diet in the Middle Ages was far different from the one we eat today. Ask students to research the food and drink nobility consumed and then find out what peasants ate. How were the diets similar? How were they different? According to today's standards, which group had the healthier diet?

5 ***From Page to Squire to Knight*** Ask your students to research the extensive training required to become a knight. Then have them prepare sequential cartoons or flip books showing how a young man was led from one step to the next until he was knighted.

Name _____ Date _____

Create Your Own Coat of Arms

There are very specific rules for designing a coat of arms.

1. Partition the background with lines. You may use any of the designs pictured in the margins or create a design of your own.
2. Choose a combination of the following colors: black, green, red, purple, gold or silver to color in your background.
3. Draw a fanciful animal as part of your design.
4. Complete your coat of arms with any personal or family symbols.

Teaching the Middle Ages With Magnificent Art Masterpieces
Scholastic Professional Books

Chess: A Medieval Game of Strategy

Chess has been popular in Europe since the 11th century. It was brought back from the East by the Crusaders. Originally, chess was played as an exercise in military strategy because the goal of the game is to take over the board by defeating the enemy king. All the chess pieces represent medieval characters.

In the boxes below, design the following chess pieces: king, queen, castle, bishop, knight, and pawn.

King	Queen	Castle
Bishop	Knight	Pawn

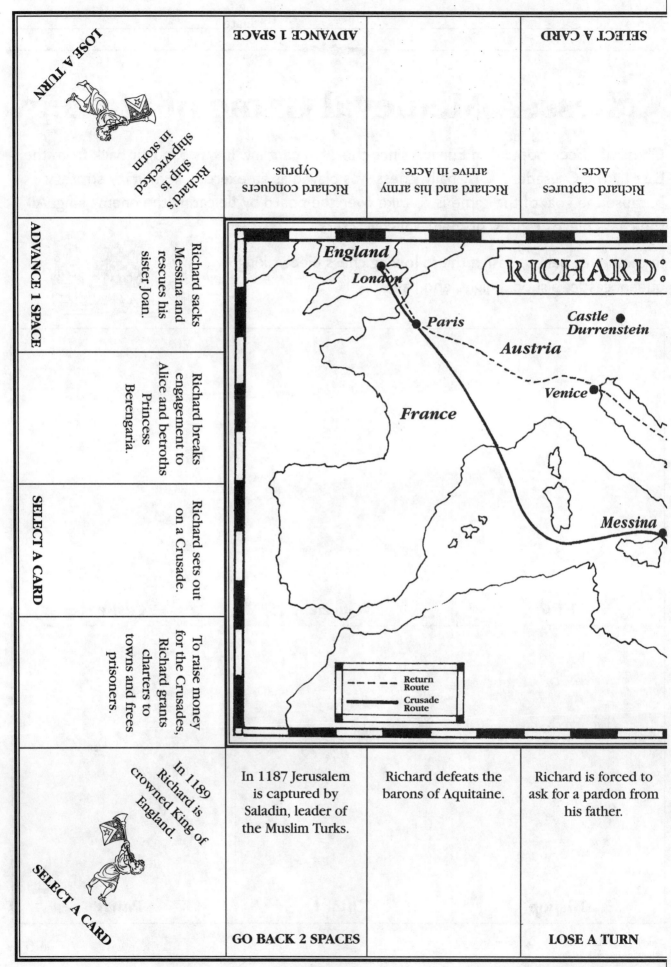

SELECT A CARD

LOSE A TURN

ADVANCE 1 SPACE

SELECT A CARD

Richard captures Acre.

Richard and his army arrive in Acre.

Richard conquers Cyprus.

Richard's ship is shipwrecked in storm.

ADVANCE 1 SPACE

Richard sacks Messina and rescues his sister Joan.

Richard breaks engagement to Alice and betroths Princess Berengaria.

SELECT A CARD

Richard sets out on a Crusade.

To raise money for the Crusades, Richard grants charters to towns and frees prisoners.

In 1189 Richard is crowned King of England.

SELECT A CARD

In 1187 Jerusalem is captured by Saladin, leader of the Muslim Turks.

GO BACK 2 SPACES

Richard defeats the barons of Aquitaine.

Richard is forced to ask for a pardon from his father.

LOSE A TURN

RICHARD:

England
London
Paris
France
Austria
Castle Durrenstein
Venice
Messina

Return Route
Crusade Route

Yea or Nay

From hilltop Richard views Jerusalem.

Richard insults his ally, Duke Leopold of Austria.

Richard realizes he can't hold Jerusalem.

SELECT A CARD

Richard signs three-year truce with Saladin.

Yea or Nay Cards

Mediterranean Sea

Cyprus

Acre
Arsuf
Jerusalem

The Holy Land

Richard sails for England, but his ship is sunk. He must return by land.

Richard travels in disguise, but is recognized by his enemy, Duke Leopold of Austria. Richard is thrown into dungeon at Durrenstein Castle.

LOSE A TURN

The minstrel Blondel discovers Richard while singing the song they had written long ago.

The barons pay Richard's ransom of 35 tons of silver.

LOSE A TURN

King Richard returns to England

FINISH

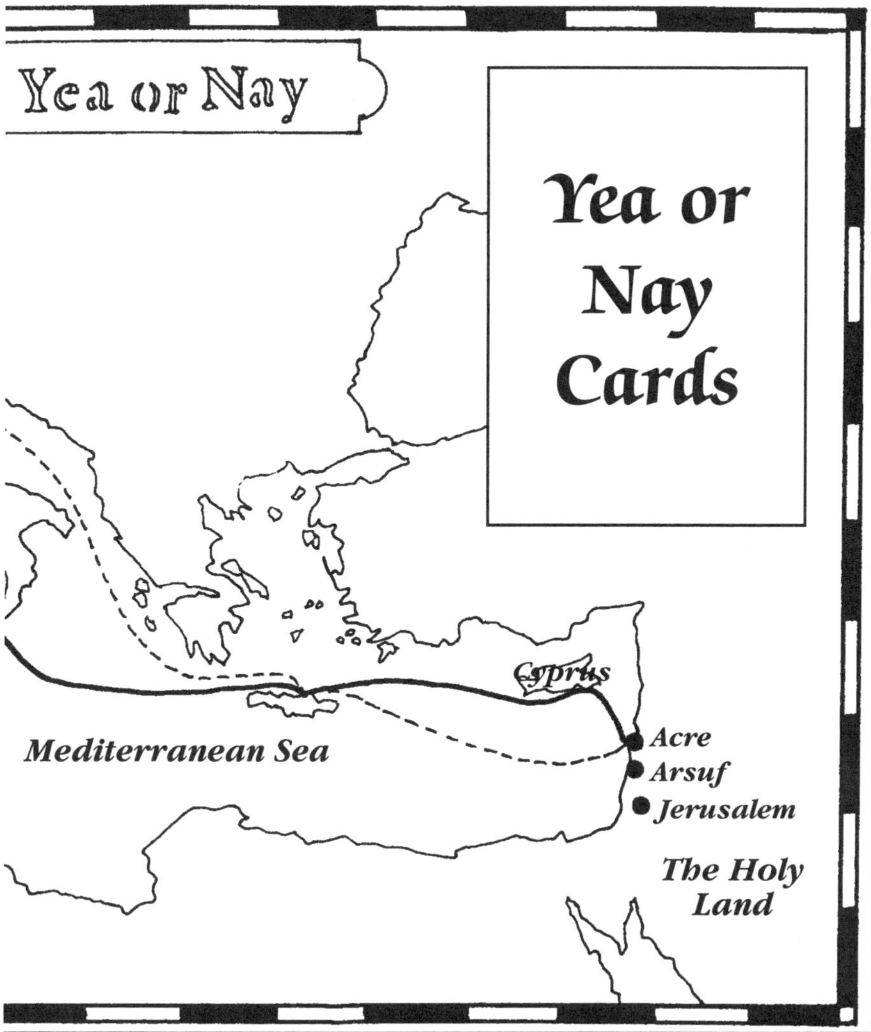

Richard goes to war against his father King Henry II.

At age 11, Richard is engaged to Princess Alice of France.

Richard goes to France to receive a knight's education.

SELECT A CARD

START

Game
Richard: Yea or Nay?

Richard the Lionhearted (1157–1199) was nicknamed "Richard, Yea or Nay" because he made decisions quickly and stubbornly held on to them. In this game you can relive Richard's exciting adventures as he becomes King of England, leads the Crusades to the Holy Land, and finally returns home.

PREPARATION

1. Reproduce the game-board pages and mount them side by side on a large piece of cardboard.

2. Make 3 copies of the Yea and Nay cards. Have players color and cut out the cards. Players should mix up the cards and then place the stack facedown on the game board.

3. Have players color, cut out, and paste the crowns on cardboard. The crowns are game markers for the players.

4. Each player places a marker on START.

5. Each player rolls the die. The highest number goes first, followed by players to the left.

PLAYING THE GAME

1. Each player pretends to be King Richard.

2. The first player rolls the die and moves his or her crown that number of spaces.

3. The player follows the directions that appear in the space on which he or she lands.

4. If a player lands on a YEA or NAY space, he or she draws a YEA or NAY card and follows the directions on the card. The card should then be placed at the bottom of the pile.

5. The object of the game is to be the first King Richard to return to England.

YEA OR NAY CARDS

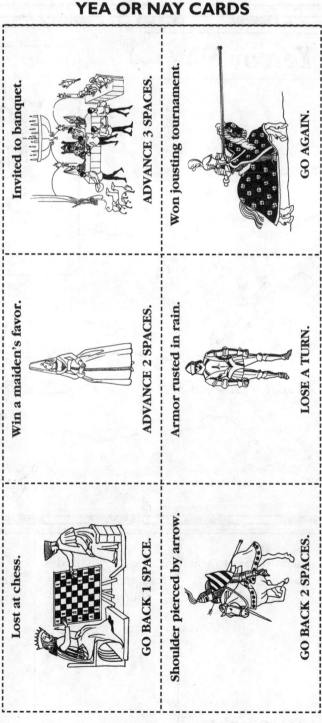

Invited to banquet. ADVANCE 3 SPACES.

Won jousting tournament. GO AGAIN.

Win a maiden's favor. ADVANCE 2 SPACES.

Armor rusted in rain. LOSE A TURN.

Lost at chess. GO BACK 1 SPACE.

Shoulder pierced by arrow. GO BACK 2 SPACES.

Teaching the Middle Ages With Magnificent Art Masterpieces
Scholastic Professional Books